Computer-assisted language learning Applications and Evaluation of their use

(Monograph)

Rakhmatova Madina Abdumumin kizi

Computer-assisted language learning Applications and Evaluation of their use

by: Rakhmatova Madina Abdumumin kizi

Edition: November '2025

Publisher:

Taemeer Publications LLC (Michigan, USA / Hyderabad, India)

ISBN 978-93-6908-764-8

9 789369 087648

Book	:	**Computer-assisted language learning Applications and Evaluation of their use**
Author	:	Rakhmatova Madina Abdumumin kizi
Publisher	:	Taemeer Publications
Year	:	'2025
Pages	:	158
Title Design	:	*Taemeer Web Design*

This monograph is devoted to the role of intellectual games in the activation and acceleration of the English language learning process. The monograph aims to introduce modern language learning opportunities that serve to activate the educational process and activities, and to develop the skills of teaching using games.

Reviewer:

Dustnazar Khimmataliev, Professor of the Department of Pedagogy and Management, Chirchik state pedagogical university

Nargiza Burieva, Associate professor, PhD on philological sciences of Jizzakh state pedagogical university

CONTENTS

INTRODUCTION

Education technologies were one of the most important developments in the second half of the twentieth century. The world's most developed areas Computers, which first appeared in schools in the late 1950s in industrialized countries, are currently evolving on a daily basis around the globe. Today, they've gotten more powerful, quicker, easier to use, more convenient, and less expensive, and they've gotten more powerful, faster, easier to use, more convenient, and less expensive. They can also analyze and store a lot more data. Computer peripherals such as hard disks, CDROMs, laser disks, and printers have also advanced swiftly. Using, in addition to characters, a computer software may handle sound, graphics, and video.

Computer-mediated communication and the Internet altered the use of computers for language acquisition at the end of the twentieth century. Computers are now used for more than only data processing and presentation; they are now used for data processing and communication. With the help of the Internet, language learners can now communicate with others or speakers of the target language from all over the world at the same time. Nonetheless, as Dhaif (1989) believes, computers will never be able to replace a "live" teacher, particularly in language classes where reciprocal communication is emphasized. It can simply serve as a teacher's aid when teaching a second or foreign language.

Aside from the standard grammar book and dictionary, there is a vast array of foreign language materials available nowadays. Course books, workbooks, programmed courses, cue carts, charts, news s, posters, image cards, and cutouts are examples of these resources. Other media, such as radio, television, slides, OHP, video tapes, games, toys, and realia, as well as computers, multi-media, and the Internet, are used[1] to supplement them.

Computer assisted language learning (CALL) workstations have taken over language laboratories that were established in the 1970s under the influence of the Audiolingual Method. "Word processors on microcomputers complement audio equipment, allowing interactive education of all four language skills: reading, listening, speaking, and writing." 377 (Crystal, 1987). Today, a wide range of FLT exercises, such as sentence restructuring, spelling checks, translation checks, dictation tasks, and cloze exams, may be computationally controlled

---

[1] Chiu, T.-L., Liou, H.-C. *et al.* (2007) A study of web-based oral activities enhanced by automatic speech recognition for EFL college learning. *Computer-Assisted Language Learning* 20(3): 209–33.

using texts displayed on the screen, according to Crystal.

Many studies consider CALL as an innovation (Albirini, 2006; Samak, 2006; Bax, 2003). Rogers (2003) defines innovation as 'an idea, a practice, or an object that is perceived as new by individuals or other units of adoption' (p. 11), while diffusion is defined as 'the process through which an innovation is communicated through certain channels over time among the members of a social system' (p.12). In his theory, Diffusion of Innovation, Rogers (2003) states that understanding the culture and local environment is important to understanding how the technology introduced can be adopted.

The adoption and integration of CALL is more than just buying computer hardware and software and making them available for teachers in schools. It is important to understand the surrounding context that helps to form the influences of these technologies on teaching and learning. As ELT programmes are not isolated from the educational context in which they are implemented, it is important to examine issues surrounding technology use, including institutional support, teachers' beliefs, and social factors as well as other issues that may stand in the way of integrating and adopting technology into these programmes (Al-Kahtani, 2004).

There are a variety of factors, both overt and covert, that affect the use and adoption of CALL in education (Elsaadani, 2013; Al-Kahtani, 2011); such factors, which affect ICT use in classrooms are termed 'extrinsic and intrinsic'. Extrinsic barriers, according to Ertmer (1999), are first-order barriers. These barriers include accessibility and time, support, and training. Intrinsic barriers are categorised as second-order barriers, which include attitudes and views, practices, and opposition. According to Al-Ruz and Khasawneh

(2011), the external or overt factors, which affect ICT adoption in education, include accessibility to computers and essential software, shortage of time for planning courses, technical, and administrative support. Numerous scholars (Lin *et al.,* 2012; Sang *et al.,* 2011; Tezci, 2011; Pelgrum, 2001) describe internal or covert factors as teacher attitudes, assurance, and faith in computer use. The features of internal (covert) factors are less apparent than external (overt) factors, which are more easily identifiable. However, many researchers believe that the attitude of teachers plays a very significant role in determining the instructional choices and utilising technology in the classroom (Elsaadani, 2013; Cox *et al.,* 2003; Pajares, 1992)[2].

Rogers (2003) states that there are several factors affecting individual adoption and attitudes

[2] Chiu, T.-L., Liou, H.-C. *et al.* (2007) A study of web-based oral activities enhanced by automatic speech recognition for EFL college learning. *Computer-Assisted Language Learning* 20(3): 209–33.

towards an innovation, which reflect on whether the innovation will be rejected or adopted. In the educational context of innovations designed for educational purposes, teachers are assumed to be major stakeholders in making such adoption decisions (Spiegel, 2001).

The Education Ministry had a ten-year (2004/2014) plan to reform the education system. The funding to the education sector has increased radically from SR 105 billion in 2008, SR 122 billion in 2009, SR 137 billion in 2010, and SR 150 billion in 2011 to the highest amount ever of SR 204 billion in 2012 (Mohammed, 2013).

Moreover, around 25 per cent of the total Saudi Arabia budget for 2015 was given to the Ministry of education (around SR 179 billion), which added to the already substantial funding being given to the Ministry of education towards the integrating of technology in the education and improvement of ICT facilities (Alenzi, 2015).

Public education was also improved by revising the curriculum and introducing electronic devices to facilitate teaching. This project also introduced training and progressive programmes for educators to ensure sufficient use of ICT in education (Tatweer, 2011). Recently, on 25 April 2016, the government announced the new *Vision 20* (2016), which promises many changes in education and transparency in the follow-up of programmes launched to improve 7

literacy. The 2016 statistics of the MOE shown in the table below indicate the number of elementary and secondary schools in the country.

In fact, **the subject matter** of this work is necessary to address the issue of learner variability. For some time now, it has been recognized that the educational paradigm "one size fits all" is not the right approach when dealing with a heterogeneous population of learners, as learners may differ in a number of characteristics and individual traits, which makes each learner's approach to learning unique.

The aim of the research is to find ways for using computers for the purpose of teaching and learning the language.

Coming out of this aim the **following tasks** were put forward:

1. to enable the student to become a critical and competent communicator
2. to gain proficiency in an additional language
3. to detect **the** effect of **using** Computer Assisted

The object of the research is **Evaluating** the nature and extent of the influence of **Computer Assisted Language Learning** (CALL) on the quality of language learning

The subject of investigation is the study

branch dealing with the application of technologies to language learning and teaching..

Theoretical value of the work is an in-depth study and evaluation analysis of the effects of the computer-assisted language teaching method.

Practical value of the work is that the material and the results of the work can be used presents a questionnaire study to help understand practices with computers in terms of learning English among Uzbekistan university students

Methods of investigation. The following methods of investigation have been applied in the present scientific work: descriptive method, contextual and stylistic analysis.

The novelty of the research to teaching and learning in which the computer and computer-based resources such as the Internet are used to present, reinforce and assess material to be learned. It usually includes a substantial interactive element..

The structure of this work is as follows: introduction, two chapters, four paragraphs, conclusion, glossary and the list of used literatures.

Introduction presents the aim, methods, theoretical and practical values of the work.

Chapter I studies the theoretical point of the chosen topic. This part deals with Computer-assisted language learning applications methodology, the internet and multimedia, a systematic evaluation framework for computer-assisted language learning and types of evaluations

Chapter II gives a practical usage of computer- assisted language learning in classrom. It consists of the eight generic CALL applications, Criteria language teachers use when selecting computer-assisted language learning technologies

Conclusion comprises the most sufficient results of the present work.

Glossary presents a short idea of the research.

The list of used literature gives the list of scientific and literary source, and internet sites.

CHAPTER I. COMPUTER ASSISTED LANGUAGE LEARNING

1.1. A systematic evaluation framework for computer-assisted language learning

Searching prestigious Computer-assisted Language Learning (CALL) journals for references to key publications and authors in the field of evaluation yields a short list. The American Journal of Evaluation—the flagship journal of the American Evaluation Association—is only cited once in both the CALICO Journal and Language Learning and Technology (Blyth & Davis, 2007). Only two articles in these journals have cited Robert Stake, Robert Yin, Daniel Stufflebeam, Michael Scriven, or Michael Patton, five of the most influential evaluators of our generation. Prestigious journals in Computer-assisted Language Learning (CALL) lacked references to formal evaluation literature, which provides a wealth of information regarding effective evaluation processes. We reviewed evaluation frameworks prominent in CALL and literature in formal evaluation. A comparison of the CALL evaluation with formal evaluation showed some overlapping tasks between the two and some gaps in CALL evaluation. Practices and insights from the field of evaluation would benefit CALL rese[3]archers and practitioners with regard to conducting systematic evaluations that report evaluation findings that other researchers and practitioners find useful. The proposed evaluation framework includes common evaluation tasks conducted by evaluators in the field of formal evaluation to produce a workflow model for designing and conducting evaluations in CALL.

---

[3] Chapelle, C. (1998) Multimedia call: lessons to be learned from research on instructed SLA. *Language Learning and Technology* 2(1): 22–34.

Implications for CALL evaluators and other stakeholders indicate several areas for improvement in CALL evaluation.

Searching prestigious CALL journals for reference to key publications and authors in the field of evaluation yields a short list. The American Journal of Evaluation—the flagship journal of the American Evaluation Association—is only cited once in both CALICO Journal and Language Learning and Technology (Blyth & Davis, 2007). Only two articles in these journals have cited Robert Stake, Robert Yin, Daniel Stufflebeam, Michael Scriven, or Michael Patton, five of the most influential evaluators of our generation. Whereas now it seems largely ignored,

the field of evaluation could provide valuable insight to CALL researchers and practitioners with regard to conducting systematic evaluations that report evaluation findings that other researchers and practitioners find useful. Chapelle (2010) stated that "the amount of published work on materials evaluation [in second language learning (SLL)] is surprisingly small in view of the impact that materials have in the instructional process" (p. 67). However, a few authors have provided guidelines for evaluation of instructional materials in SLL (Cunningsworth, 1984; Sheldon, 1988; Skierso, 1991; Tomlinson, 2003). Additionally, many prominent authors in CALL have proposed evaluation frameworks for evaluating CALL (Beatty, 2010; Burston, 2003; Chapelle, 2001, 2007, 2010; Garrett, 2009; Hubbard, 1988, 1996, 2006, 2011; Levy & Stockwell, 2006; Reeder, Heift, Roche, Tabyanian, Schlickau, & Golz, 2004; Susser, 2001; Villada, 2009). While these frameworks have their strengths, the systematic approach and practices of formal evaluators such as those of the American Evaluation Association

(AEA), would help CALL evaluators design and conduct evaluations that are methodologically similar to formal evaluations, while maintaining the diversity offered by these various frameworks.

A framework for conducting evaluation of CALL must provide systematic steps that are based on proven evaluation practices. A systematic approach to designing and conducting quality evaluations would produce a body of transferable and usable data to help inform developers, researchers, practitioners, and students. Prior to the Henry Ford's Model T, several inventors had developed machine-driven wheeled vehicles. Ford realized that in order to popularize such a vehicle, it needed to meet the needs of the consumers and be affordable. Soon after the success of Ford motor vehicles, others entrepreneurs began to create competing products that borrowed and improved upon Ford's technologies. Ford, in turn, made an even better product based on the consumers' interest in competing products. Today we still see this constant improvement of vehicles, yet none would argue that the Model T was ineffective or useless. Rather, the Model T was a marvel of its time and paved the way for innovation in transportation.

CALL evaluation is similar to the early pre-Model T vehicles. Evaluation in CALL has added to other fields and improved the quality of evaluation of non computer-based materials in second language learning. CALL evaluation can be further enhanced by the field of formal evaluation. In this article, we propose a conceptual framework for designing and conducting evaluations in CALL that builds on the works of Hubbard (1987, 1988, 1996, 2006), Chapelle 5 (1999, 2001, 2007, 2010) and others (Beatty, 2010; Burston, 2003; Levy & Stockwell,

2006;

Reeder et al., 2004; Susser, 2001; Villada, 2009) and incorporates literature from the field of evaluation. The purpose of the conceptual framework is to answer the following question: What is an appropriate systematic approach for conducting evaluations in CALL?

The two prominent frameworks by Hubbard (1987, 1988, 1996, 2006, 2011) and Chapelle (2001, 2007, 2011) provided for limited suggestions for determining criteria by which to judge their proposed evaluand. Hubbard suggested looking at technical considerations, operational descriptions, teacher fit, learner fit, and implementation. Burston's (2003) suggestions mimicked Hubbard's, but he also suggested that all software be both pedagogically valid and adaptable to the curriculum as well as efficient, effective, and pedagogically innovative. Both Hubbard and

Burston inferred that these criteria are sufficient for evaluation of software. While they may serve as a starting point, evaluations that follow these guidelines lack the consideration of stakeholder values and may fail to address the intended outcomes of the evaluation. Chapelle (2001) emphasized that "evaluation criteria should incorporate findings and theory-based speculation about ideal conditions for SLA" (p. 52). As mentioned earlier, the 30 focus of her evaluation framework was actual CALL tasks. While these overlap with some of Hubbard's (1987, 1988, 1996, 2006, 2011) criteria, the focus revolves more around language learning. With regard to this, Reeder et al. (2004) argued that there is a lack of identified criteria that addresses both learning outcomes and learning processes. They also stated that evaluative criteria often fail to connect to design and instructional methodologies. While Chapelle's (2001) criteria may help evaluators and stakeholders determine their own evaluative criteria, selecting criteria based on the values of evaluators is curiously absent. Considering the desired outcomes of the evaluand and incorporating them with stakeholders' values may address the concerns of Reeder et al. (2004). In SLL, Tomlinson (2003) who referred to materials evaluation generally and not specifically to CALL, identified 19 principles for materials developme[4]nt (p. 21-22). These principles are founded in research and his own experience. These work well as criteria in the materials' subsequent evaluation. One possible strength of this list is that it may be representative of the values of CALL practitioners and stakeholders alike. Obviously, evaluating materials to ensure that they meet all possible

---

[4] Chapelle, C., Jamieson, J. and Park, Y. (1996) Second language classroom research traditions: how does CALL fit? In Pennington, M. (ed.), *The Power of CALL*. Houston, TX: Athelstan: 33–53.

criteria would be a large undertaking and may not even be practical, but the point is clear. Evaluation seeks to determine what should be. By clearly articulating the criteria or standards by which the evaluand will be measured, evaluators can have a directed study that lends itself to clear and defensible results, leading to clear and defensible decisions. Only by considering the intended evaluand, outcomes, and stakeholders' values can effective criteria be selected and used in the evaluation process.

Methodology This review of the literature followed Machi and McEvoy's (2010) six steps for producing a literature review: selecting a topic, searching the literature, developing an argument, surveying the literature, critiquing the literature, and writing the review. When looking at literature, we decided to search for journal articles and key authors in the Linguistics Language Behavior Abstracts (LLBA) database

because it provides the richest search options for CALL
when compared with Educational Resources Information Center (ERIC). Next, we searched for literature on evaluation processes and standards. ERIC provided these three thesaurus terms: evaluation, evaluation methods, and evaluation research. A search for program evaluation standards provided several articles that address the implementation of the standards. Looking for literature regarding evaluation processes, tasks, and standards in ERIC was much less successful.

Evaluation Defined and Described - *Evaluation* is a systematic process that seeks to determine the value, worth, importance, significance, or merit of an object, person, or activity (Stake & Schwandt, 2006; Yarbrough, Shulha, Hopson, & Caruthers, 2010). At the core of evaluation, evaluators seek to gather and interpret data that helps us make judgments about the evaluated (Nunan, 1992). These judgments are arrived at by the interpretation of data, whether quantitative, qualitative, or both. Systematic evaluation methodologies are similar to research methodologies. In fact, Nunan (1992) declared, "I believe that evaluations, incorporating as they do questions, data and interpretation, are a form of research" (p. 184). Levy and Stockwell (2006) referred to this as the research-evaluation nexus. However, there are notable differences in purpose between evaluation and research. The aim of most research is to produce "credible, generalizable knowledge about the nature of the world around us" whereas "evaluations help stakeholders answer specific questions or make decisions . . . [and] investigate such things as a program's development, processes, theory, viability, outcomes and impact" (Yarbrough, Shulha, Hopson, Caruthers, 2010, p. xxv). Research and evaluation not only differ in purpose, but they also have different audiences. Research, for example, is directed to academic peers interested in

generalizable results while evaluation is directed to specific stakeholders within a specified context. In defining evaluation, it is also important to recognize its relationship to assessment and measurement. Nunan (1992) pointed out that much of the literature confused the terms assessment and evaluation. In education, assessment is a type of evaluation that seeks to 7 determine the learning of students in formative or summative ways. Educational measurement is the use of assessment data to draw conclusions about students' and their abilities. In other words, assessment and measurement both fall under the broader category of evaluation.

The proposed framework for conducting evaluations has several implications for CALL evaluators. Many of these mark a significant change from current practices. For example, the suggested framework includes explicitly setting and reporting evaluation criteria and conducting a metaevaluation. Other evaluation tasks outlined may serve to reinforce already accepted practices such as identifying stakeholders and including them in designing the evaluation. These implications may also be helpful for stakeholders other than the evaluator. Stakeholders who are well informed about conducting reliable and valid evaluations can help evaluators conduct welldesigned evaluations. Administrators, publishers, designers, and others should strongly consider the following implications. Doing so will result in evaluations that are more systematic, thorough, and useful. Applying the evaluation tasks outlined in this paper might lead to the following suggestions for improving CALL evaluations. The list includes several variations from common trends in CALL evaluation to incorporate more practices from formal evaluators.

However, it is also important to note that assessment and measurement do not exclusively belong to evaluation–both are used in research as well.

The term *formal evaluation* is used throughout the article to represent the field of professional evaluation—it refers to the ideals, principles, standards and practices of *formal evaluators*. The evaluation field does not belong to one specific group or domain, rather it refers to the professional practice of formal evaluation.

Analysis of Popular CALL Frameworks. The most popular evaluation frameworks in CALL have been posited by Hubbard (1987, 1988, 1996, 2006, 2011) and Chapelle (2001), each of which has strengths and weaknesses. In the following paragraphs we provide an overview of Hubbard's and Chapelle's frameworks. To analyze the frameworks, we took each of the principles identified in the evaluation literature as key for successful evaluations and then considered how and in what ways each principle applied to the Chapelle and Hubbard frameworks. We noted similarities and overlapping ideas. From this analysis process we created a list of evaluation principles and ideas for how they could be 8 realized in CALL. We then conducted a reliability check by asking two professional evaluators and two CALL scholars to review the framework for deficiencies, overlapping ideas, and clarity.

Hubbard's Framework. We will first look at Hubbard's (2011) latest publication on his framework. As with his previous publications regarding evaluation, Hubbard provides some background information about evaluation of computer-assisted language learning software in which he can situate his proposed evaluation framework. From the onset he mentions four distinct purposes of CALL evaluation: selection for use in a course, selection for use in self-access environments or for other instructors, published reviews, and feedback during the development process. Hubbard presented these purposes not as a comprehensive list but as a specific subset to which his framework can be applied. Hubbard narrowed the list of evaluation approaches or methodologies to three specific types: checklists, methodological frameworks, and SLA research. Checklists are essentially a combination of criteria that evaluators review and to which they assign some type of score using a Likert scale or other rating systems. While this is a common methodology used to evaluate CALL, in many cases it assumes that the evaluation criteria is *one size fits all*. Evaluators can change and alter a checklist to match the criteria specified by stakeholders, but the use of checklists as an approach or *methodology* for CALL evaluation may be confounded by its overlap with evaluation *criteria*. These checklists tend to be a list of evaluation criteria and may not provide adequate methodological concerns to CALL evaluation, omitting key procedures in the evaluation process. The other two approaches mentioned are not exempt from similar phenomena. Methodological frameworks, as described by Hubbard, allow evaluators to form their own 9 questions. In this regard, the evaluator may be the sole stakeholder. This may be a limitation for evaluators with little experience who rely on CALL evaluation frameworks such as this one to guide their evaluation. Thus, it could become increasingly easy for evaluators to neglect potential stakeholders. Hubbard (1988) based his original framework on the works of Phillips (1985) and Richards and Rogers (1982). While the confusion between criteria and methodologies in Hubbard's framework is not as prominent as it is with checklists, evaluators may interpret his suggestions as prescribed criteria.

Maxis has produced many Sim games for environments ranging from jungles to other planets. The most interesting recent development has been the release of a program called *The Sims*. In this game, users create characters and their families, build homes and cater to their needs (e.g. hunger). If one clicks on a fridge, the character on screen will go to the fridge and prepare a meal for himself/herself. Many users model their own families and homes in the program.

A more recent development is *Spore*, a game in which a player controls the development of a single-celled organism into a complex thinking being, ostensibly controlling the creature's evolution. The game has been criticized for placing entertainment far above sound scientific principles but it is an example of a game that involves a great deal of reading and discussion if played with more than one person.

Chappelle's Framework. Chapelle's (2001) framework for evaluation varies from Hubbard's. From the outset, it is clear that she did not limit the types of evaluands as strictly as Hubbard. Her framework is broad enough to consider CALL software, teacher-planned CALL activities, and learners' performance during CALL activities. She also lists standards for selecting the evaluation criteria and even suggests some specific criteria. Chapelle (2001) discussed the importance of criteria based in SLA research and stated that, "learning language potential should be the central criterion in the evaluation of CALL" (p. 52). She also lists learner fit, meaning focus, authenticity, positive impact, and practicality as criteria to be considered in CALL evaluations. Chapelle suggests that CALL evaluations should be looked at from two perspectives: (a) a judgmental analysis of CALL software and activities and (b) an empirical analysis of the learner's performance. In many ways, this could be a recommendation for various research methodologies. She implied that the evaluand dictates, at least to some degree, the type of analysis that should be done in an evaluation. Table 1 shows three types of analyses with her suggested evaluand (object of evaluation), question, and evaluation type (method of evaluation) for each analysis. While some CALL evaluands would appear to be best evaluated qualitatively and others quantitatively, this too may be limiting. Rather than basing the type of approach on the nature of the evaluand, it should be based on a series of factors including the nature of the evaluand, the evaluation questions, and the evaluation criteria. For example, when considering the evaluation of a multiple-choice test, evaluators might think that using a quantitative approach would work best. While this may be true if the questions focus on the data from test scores and item analyses, qualitative approaches shouldn't be ignored. If the primary evaluation question focuses on learner perception of the test, qualitative ethodologies may be more effective. Hubbard (2011) and Chapelle's (2001) frameworks differ in their focus, with Hubbard emphasizing process, including its parts and the details and specific suggestions for each step. For example, he spelled out various purposes of a CALL evaluation. Chapelle on the other hand focused less on creating a procedural map for conducting evaluations and more on purpose, criteria, and methodologies.

To summarize, Chappelle's framework may be effective in certain circumstances, particularly those evaluating CALL for language issues, but it may not be helpful when considering other non-SLA issues, such as financial or hardware requirements. Following Chappelle's framework may also generate evaluations that do not consider the values of 13 underrepresented stakeholders such as software developers and program administrators. Evaluators who are considering non-SLA issues, such as the finances, infrastructure, or other administrative aspects would benefit from a framework that allows for other considerations such as financial issues or hardware requirements.

Hubbard claimed that his framework could be adapted toward aspects of CALL outside of courseware and websites. However, it is only focused on these two evaluands. Chapelle's suggested evaluands are placed on a continuum ranging from the evaluation of a complete course to technology used in a traditional face-to-face learning. While the spectrum allows for a wide range of evaluands, it may exclude other CALL tools or activities. The continuum focuses on technology as used in the context of a course, whether in face-to-face or online environments. Other possible evaluands may include technologies and activities that learners engage in independent of formal class settings.

Although Hubbard briefly mentions developers as stakeholders when evaluating developing products, he limits stakeholders to teachers and learners. While in many cases these are the more prominent, there are always other stakeholders to consider. Each evaluation may have different stakeholders whose input should be considered. For example, school administrators, parents, and developers may be vital and perhaps underrepresented groups that can help increase the completeness as well as the validity of the evaluation. Chapelle included a lengthy list of types of evaluations and possible audiences that may also be counted as stakeholders. This list can serve as both a list of audiences to whom evaluations might be reported as well as list of possible stakeholders.

One strength of Hubbard's framework is the extensive list of criteria to be considered when evaluating CALL courseware and websites. However, this is not an exhaustive list and should only be a starting point. The suggestions are specific to courseware and website evaluations, but there may be other criteria important to stakeholders.

Additionally, there are no suggestions for criteria for evaluating CALL activities or even hardware used in language learning.

While Chapelle made no explicit mention of evaluation purposes, her continuum of evaluands (ranging from the evaluation of a complete course to technology used in a traditional face-to-face learning) may indicate implied purposes similar to those Hubbard mentioned: selecting technology for a course, selection for self-access or other instructor use, and published reviews.

However, he also pointed out that in some situations you may define evaluation or research questions, select methods to collect data, and then return to the question in order to tweak it to work better with the chosen methods. Figure 3 shows that each of the previous tasks are intertwined and culminate in the questions asked about the evaluation. Similarly, evaluators may need to return to the previous evaluation tasks after asking the research or evaluation questions. In cooperation with stakeholders, evaluators may need to 32 reconsider evaluation criteria and make any necessary changes to the criteria or the question to make sure that each part of the evaluation matches the others. In order to have questions that match the evaluation, evaluators must work with stakeholders to help arrive at overall evaluation questions. What do we (the evaluators and stakeholders) want to know about the evaluand? What questions do we need to ask to achieve our purpose? In many ways, the process of determining appropriate and evaluable questions resembles the same process that researchers undertake when asking research questions. It is essential that evaluators and stakeholders realize the connectivity among the first five evaluation tasks and developing evaluation questions. In concert, those five tasks help the development of effective evaluation questions, which in turn may require returning to those same five tasks.

1.2. Types of Evaluations

Unlike many of the evaluation types used by formal evaluators, Hubbard's evaluation types seemed to be tied to the data collection methods rather than the purpose of the evaluation. Hubbard (2011) cited Levy and Stockwell's (2006) three types of courseware evaluation in CALL: checklists and forms, methodological frameworks, and SLA-based approaches. Formal evaluators may adopt an evaluation type based on the purpose of the evaluation, and while some types may favor a particular type of data collection, they are not limited by it. For example, formal evaluators use quantitative, qualitative, and mixed methods to collect and analyze data gathered during an evaluation.

While Chapelle (2001) did not specify any specific type of evaluation, she did group evaluations into three distinct categories. She mentioned evaluations that are based on teachers' judgment, those that are focused on the analysis of performance data, and then evaluations that may be a synthesis of the two former types. These seem to be largely based in the participants of the evaluations—teachers and students.

Both Hubbard and Chappelle grouped the creation of evaluation questions with other formal evaluation tasks. Hubbard suggested that the questions be connected to data collection methods while Chapelle implied the use of research questions. Both have merit and are essential areas to consider when drafting evaluation questions, but evaluation questions come through information from stakeholders and the identification of the evaluand, criteria, purpose, and type of evaluation.

As mentioned previously, Hubbard's mixed types of evaluation with types of data collection. In contrast, Chapelle (2001) suggested using research methodologies to collect data to be used in evaluations. She mentioned qualitative and quantitative approaches. She discussed the use of ethnographies, case studies, interaction analyses, discourse analyses, and both experimental and quasi-experimental methodologies. Depending on the questions asked about the evaluand, evaluators can choose a methodology that would best lend itself to the collection of valid and reliable data.

In Hubbard's framework, the method for reporting findings and implications is linked to the evaluation's purpose. For example, the findings of a courseware evaluation may only be reported to the teacher and perhaps the students. When writing a review of software or a website, the findings may be published in a journal or website. His suggested reporting venues with their strong connection to evaluation purposes were indeed helpful, but should not be seen as the only ones possible. Chapelle largely discussed her list of possible stakeholders as possible audiences, but provided little elaboration. In addition to the suggested venues an audience for evaluation reports, there are several venues for reporting findings, and evaluators should be encouraged to find ways to share results.

The evaluand is the object, person, or activity being evaluated. Program evaluation is often used to discuss evaluands that include educational programs, policies, or projects. In order to conduct an evaluation, evaluators need to identify what the evaluand is and what the evaluand should be. Identifying the evaluand is not always an easy process and often times there are several evaluands that can be explored. Most CALL practitioners and researchers recognize two types of evaluands: materials and activities.

Hubbard's (1988, 1996, 2006, 2011) framework focused on tools such as courseware and websites as evaluands. Levy and Stockwell (2006) suggested software, online courses, websites, computer-mediated communication, and combinations of elements (i.e., learning management systems) as evaluands. Reeder et al. (2004) suggested three types of software that could be the object of evaluations: microcosm situations, micro ethnographies, and online programs. Chapelle's (2001, 2010) guidelines for evaluating CALL tended to focus on activities as evaluands. She later identified what is taught in a complete course, what is taught through technology in a complete course, and what is taught through technology as three evaluation targets. She defined a complete course as one that is web-delivered or technology based. By looking at what is taught through technology in a complete course, she suggested that evaluators look at a subset of the total course objectives as the evaluand. What is taught through technology refers to technology that is used to enhance (Chapelle, 2007). Because the most common frameworks for CALL evaluation focus on materials and activities, many of the published evaluations focus on these two evaluands.

Stakeholders are all those who have some interest in the evaluand and by extension the evaluation. In educational settings, students, teachers, and administrators are the most frequently identified stakeholders. Often evaluators overlook curriculum and materials developers, parents, funding agencies, and other members of the community. Evaluators are sometimes overlooked as stakeholders, but indeed become an interested party in the evaluand when conducting an evaluation (Sechrest, Babcock, & Smith, 1993). They bring expertise and unique views to the evaluation design that can help other stakeholders in the development of quality evaluations.

Carefully identified stakeholders can provide essential information about the evaluand and help shape the evaluation in such a way that it becomes useful to all those invested.Key authors in CALL have identified possible stakeholders for CALL evaluations. Levy and Stockwell (2006) discussed how designers and developers of CALL materials are evaluators. They pointed out that many of the published CALL research articles focus on tools and their evaluation. They stated, "the designer-evaluator perspective is a very important one incontemporary CALL evaluation" (p. 52). Chapelle (2001) argued that due to the complexity of CALL evaluation, all those who use CALL should be involved in the evaluation process. In a later article, Chapelle (2007) discussed audiences for evaluations. Regardless of the differences between stakeholders and audience, there is some overlap. She identified insiders, informed critics, and outsiders as three separate audiences. Insiders include software developers and other CALL researchers. Other teachers, learners, other applied linguists, and program decision makers are among the informed critics. Outsiders may overlap with critics and include program and policy decision makers. Hubbard (1988, 1996, 2006, 2011) gave high priority to teachers and learners as stakeholders. While these prominent figures in the field have identified a myriad of possible stakeholders, many published evaluations still focus on only one or two groups of stakeholders.

Villada's (2009) proposed interpretive evaluation framework focused on multivocality as one of its main tenets. He defined multivocality as multiple voices or perspectives. Of the 24 articles on evaluations that he reviewed, 14 only addressed. Guba and Lincoln (1981) stated that, "the evaluator has a duty to identify all audiences, to do his best to determine what their concerns

and issues are, and to honor and respond to those concerns and issues" (p. 306). CALL evaluation frameworks should incorporate the voices of all stakeholders
when possible.

There are various reasons for conducting an evaluation. With the evaluand in mind and in collaboration with stakeholders, evaluators should define a clear purpose for conducting the evaluation and ask detailed questions to guide the rest of the process. CALL scholars have identified some relevant evaluation purposes. Hubbard (1988, 1996, 2006, 2011) suggested the following possible purposes: (a) selection for a course; (b) selection for self-access or other instructor use; (c) reviews; and (d) feedback for development. Levy and Stockwell (2006) suggested that investigating "one of the unique, defining features of CALL" (p. 43). They also discussed purposes such as seeing if CALL materials are working as they should, assessing value and effectiveness of CALL materials, and learning about viability and effectiveness of specific methodologies and strategies. Their review of the literature also led them to other purposes such as assessing student attitudes and perceptions, obtaining feedback from students about CALL courses and courseware, and investigating learners' views on features of the tools they are using.

The purpose of the evaluation affects evaluation that should be conducted taking into consideration other variables including the skills, qualifications, or experience of the evaluators and the interests of stakeholders. Having defined purposes that were selected by 25 stakeholders while keeping in mind the evaluation's resulting decisions strongly influence what kind of evaluation should take place. Many CALL evaluators and formal evaluators refer to evaluations as either formative or summative.

CALL evaluators have delineated other types of evaluations that are tightly connected to their evaluative purposes. Formal evaluators suggest various models for conducting evaluations. These models provide CALL with a wealth of methods and frameworks for conducting evaluations for unique purposes. As CALL evaluators shift their independent evaluation paradigms and adopt, or at the very least borrow from, models that formal evaluators use; the efficacy, efficiency, and quality of CALL evaluations may improve. First, we will look at evaluation types as generally discussed in SLL and CALL. Second, we will look at a few of the more prominent evaluation types found in formal evaluation literature.

The types of evaluations proposed in SLL and CALL materials evaluation. Tomlinson (2003) discussed three types of evaluation. As mentioned earlier, these are connected to the purposes of the evaluation. Pre-use evaluation looks at how the materials might benefit the users. Whilst-use evaluations investigate the value of the materials while they are being used. Post-use evaluation, he argued, is the "most valuable (but least administered) type of evaluation as it can measure the actual effects of materials on users" (p. 25). Chapelle (2001) described two types of CALL evaluation: judgmental and empirical. She argued that judgmental analyses examine the "characteristics of the software and the tasks" while empirical analyses are based on "data gathered to reveal the details of CALL use and learning outcomes" (p. 54). Reeder et al. (2004) promoted a similar dichotomy in evaluation calling one type introspective and the other empirical. They argued that introspective evaluations often result in completed checklists or reviews. Introspective 26 evaluations often use similar criteria and provide information about the material and are based on the reviewers' perspectives. Like Chapelle (2001, 2007), they argued that empirical evaluations involve looking at students in authentic situations. CALL authors tended to mix the *type* of evaluation with the methods for *collecting data*.

Formal evaluation literature is abundant in proposed types of evaluation. Table 3 provides brief descriptions of a selection of formal evaluation types. The purpose of describing these is to introduce specific ways to guide CALL evaluators. However, we do not provide extensive information for conducting each type of evaluation. Lynch (1996) is possibly the only author in SLL that has situated evaluation ideals in the context of language learning. He discussed the responsive model, the illumination model, and goal-free evaluation among others. Other prominent models include Stufflebeam's (2003) CIPP model that includes context, input, process, and product evaluations. Reeves and Hedberg (2003) discussed effectiveness evaluation and impact evaluation. Patton has also introduced utilization (participant-oriented) evaluation (2003, 2008) and developmental evaluation (2010).

Several of the proposed purposes for evaluation of CALL correspond well to formal evaluators use. Although we provide only a small description of each evaluation type, we also suggests some scenarios in which each evaluation may be appropriate in the context of CALL. We elaborate on a few of the types and situations in the following paragraphs. *Responsive evaluation*. For example, Stake's (1975, 2003, 2004) responsive evaluation may be suited to the evaluation of prototypes used in teaching. The nature of changing values and concerns of stakeholders can be difficult to account for, but Stake's model may be helpful in dealing with such issues. 27

Illuminative evaluation. What Chapelle (2001) and Reeder et al. (2004) called *judgmental* or *introspective evaluation* may be a closer resemblance to illuminative evaluation. However, this type of evaluation is not limited to materials as evaluands and can help evaluators conduct judgmental or introspective evaluations of activities because it also provides for the exploration of student tasks and experiences (Parlett & Hamilton, 1976). *Utilization-focused evaluation*. Utilization-focused evaluations may have a unique fit in CALL. As academic journals increasingly publish evaluations of CALL materials, editors and publishers should consider how these evaluations will actually be used by the stakeholders. Patton (2003) stated that, "Utilization-focused evaluation is concerned with how real people in the real world apply evaluation findings and experience the evaluation process. Therefore, the focus in utilization-focused evaluation is on the intended use by intended users" (p. 223). *Developmental evaluation*. The developmental evaluation model, with its affordances for complexity, is also well-suited for CALL, which in itself corporates the complexity inherent in technology use and language learning. Perhaps one application of this model could be throughout the development process of new products and even changing and evolving language learning curricula that employ or rely heavily upon CALL. These are only a few of the models that formal evaluation literature has to offer CALL. When CALL evaluators consider the various types of evaluation at their disposal, they can take advantage of tried practices by experienced evaluators, which will strengthen their evaluative skills and the evaluations that they produce. The type of evaluation is connected to its purposes and affects the questions, criteria, methods, and reporting of findings of the evaluation.

The two prominent frameworks by Hubbard (1987, 1988, 1996, 2006, 2011) and Chapelle (2001, 2007, 2011) provided for limited suggestions for determining criteria by which to judge their proposed evaluand. Hubbard suggested looking at technical considerations, operational descriptions, teacher fit, learner fit, and implementation. Burston's (2003) suggestions mimicked Hubbard's, but he also suggested that all software be both pedagogically valid and adaptable to the curriculum as well as efficient, effective, and pedagogically innovative. Both Hubbard and Burston inferred that these criteria are sufficient for evaluation of software. While they may serve as a starting point, evaluations that follow these guidelines lack the consideration of stakeholder values and may fail to address the intended outcomes of the evaluation. Chapelle (2001) emphasized that "evaluation criteria should incorporate findings and theory-based speculation about ideal conditions for SLA" (p. 52). As mentioned earlier, the 30 focus of her evaluation framework was actual CALL tasks. While these overlap with some of Hubbard's (1987, 1988, 1996, 2006, 2011) criteria, the focus revolves more around language learning. With regard to this, Reeder et al. (2004) argued that there is a lack of identified criteria that addresses both learning outcomes and learning processes. They also stated that evaluative criteria often fail to connect to design and instructional methodologies. While Chapelle's (2001) criteria may help evaluators and stakeholders determine their own evaluative criteria, selecting criteria based on the values of evaluators is curiously absent. Considering the desired outcomes of the evaluand and incorporating them with stakeholders' values may address the concerns of Reeder et al. (2004). In SLL, Tomlinson (2003) who referred to materials evaluation generally and not specifically to CALL, identified 19 principles for materials developme[5]nt (p. 21-22). These principles are founded in research and his own experience. These work well as criteria in the materials' subsequent evaluation. One possible strength of this list is that it may be representative of the values of CALL practitioners and stakeholders alike. Obviously, evaluating materials to ensure that they meet all possible criteria would be a large undertaking and may not even be practical, but the point is clear. Evaluation seeks to determine what should be. By clearly articulating the criteria or standards by which the evaluand will be measured, evaluators

---

[5] Chapelle, C., Jamieson, J. and Park, Y. (1996) Second language classroom research traditions: how does CALL fit? In Pennington, M. (ed.), *The Power of CALL*. Houston, TX: Athelstan: 33–53.

can have a directed study that lends itself to clear and defensible results, leading to clear and defensible decisions. Only by considering the intended evaluand, outcomes, and stakeholders' values can effective criteria be selected and used in the evaluation process. 31

Following the previous evaluation tasks, evaluators and stakeholders should ask questions. Figure 3 demonstrates the relationship this task has with the previous ones. With a purpose and type of evaluation in mind, a clearly identified evaluand, and set evaluation criteria, asking questions about the evaluand should be a well-informed task. *Figure 3.* Evaluation tasks with the development of evaluation questions. Stake (2010) emphasized the importance of asking questions before selecting methods to collect data. However, he also pointed out that in some situations you may define evaluation or research questions, select methods to collect data, and then return to the question in order to tweak it to work better with the chosen methods. Figure 3 shows that each of the previous tasks are intertwined and culminate in the questions asked about the evaluation—questions that drive the evaluation. Similarly, evaluators may need to return to the previous evaluation tasks after asking the research or evaluation questions. In cooperation with stakeholders, evaluators may need to 32 reconsider evaluation criteria and make any necessary changes to the criteria or the question to make sure that each part of the evaluation matches the others. In order to have questions that match the evaluation, evaluators must work with stakeholders to help arrive at overall evaluation questions. What do we (the evaluators and stakeholders) want to know about the evaluand? What questions do we need to ask to achieve our purpose? In many ways, the process of determining appropriate and evaluable questions resembles the same process that researchers undertake when asking research questions. It is essential that evaluators and stakeholders realize the connectivity among the first five evaluation tasks and developing evaluation questions. In concert, those five tasks help the development of effective evaluation questions, which in turn may require returning to those same five tasks. For example, personnel in an intensive English program (stakeholders) use a mobile application for L2 literacy (evaluand), and want to see if it leads to an increase in reading fluency over the course of a semester (criteria) to determine if they should continue using the application (purpose). The evaluators and stakeholders decide that an effectiveness evaluation (type) is best suited for this situation. With this information they develop the main evaluation question: What effect does the mobile application have on the reading fluency of students?

Evaluators commonly use checklists in judgmental evaluation of CALL materials. However, Susser (2001) suggested that the use of checklists for CALL and SLA evaluation have been criticized. He identified several areas in which various scholars described the shortcomings of checklists. Decoo (1994) questioned the accuracy, compatibility, and transferability of checklists. Squires and McDougall (1994) suggested that checklists may place too much focus on the technical features of courseware and neglect to consider pedagogical concerns. Susser (2001) referred to several experimental studies that questioned the objectivity of checklists. Similarly, he argued that some checklists may favor a particular theory of language acquisition or computer-assisted instruction. He also pointed out that the

background knowledge of those completing the checklist may affect the criticality of the reviewer and the overall accuracy of the completed checklist. Despite these arguments against checklists, Susser (2001) defended their use and explained that if they are used in the right contexts for the right purposes, checklists can be an
excellent tool. Chapelle (2001, 2007), Hubbard (1988, 1996, 2011), and Reeder et al. (2004) all acknowledged value in checklists for judgmental purposes, or in other words for describing CALL materials and activities.

Chapelle (2001, 2007) advocated that quantitative, qualitative and mixed methods approaches can be used in empirical evaluations. She connected research methodologies to evaluation. She discussed that much of the research in CALL is ased on theoretical comparison research that employs experimental and quasi-experimental designs. A 34 theoretically motivated approach to CALL evaluation may include qualitative methodologies such as ethnographies and case studies in addition to the more quantitative experimental and quasi-experimental methodologies. She also indicated that interaction and discourse analysis may be effective methodologies used in evaluation. Levy and Stockwell (2006) also mentioned how research methods may be used in evaluation when describing the evaluation-research nexus. Reeder et al. (2004) pointed out that many evaluations are based on experimental designs and that these might be problematic or at least make it difficult to determine the validity of outcomes from treatment groups. Reeves et al. (2005) argued that design research might be more effective than traditional experimental research. For example, experimental designs often do not control for all the variables and treatment groups are often unnatural and lack resemblance to a typical classroom. They also noted that when questionnaires are used to collect data from control and treatment groups, they are often narrow in their scope and any learning results not predicted and indicated in the questionnaire may be missed. Just as in research, evaluation results need to be reported. Unlike researchers who publish their work in books and academic journals, with the intention of providing generalizable or transferable findings that add to the body of research, evaluation reports might only be made available to the stakeholders. While in certain contexts a complete report with all the details may be appropriate, for many stakeholders, a brief report that includes a summary of the evaluation is often preferred. Because evaluations are extremely context dependent, they are not generalizable; their findings may, however, be transferable. Any insights gained from a specific evaluation could be used to direct evaluations of other programs and some implications might be beneficial. Sharing evaluations with other teachers, students, administrators, and additional interested parties can be helpful as it may provide insights to others beyond the stakeholders and those who commissioned the evaluation. In language programs, evaluations could be made available to others working in the program. Software evaluations are often published in journals in both print and online formats. Additionally, evaluations of CALL tools and activities could be posted to a website making them available to a wider audience. Because evaluations are not intended to be generalizable to all contexts, published evaluations should include sufficient information such as a detailed description of the evaluand, the purpose of the evaluation, and the criteria by which the evaluand was evaluated so that others can understand the context for interpreting evaluation results and can apply the findings to their own circumstances as they feel appropriate. Evaluations are only effective if they are used. Scriven (1990) argued that software developers and users need, “to be willing and able to do and use evaluation” (p. 3), and Patton 36 (2003, 2008) emphasized a utilization-focused evaluation approach for making evaluations useful to stakeholders. Beatty (2010) provided insight into the actual use of evaluations. He suggested that conducting in-house reviews by peers and making evaluations available to everyone may be one of the better approaches to creating useful evaluations. He argued that there is value in making evaluations available so they can be used by others to make conscientious decisions about the technology used. The students might evaluate software in a self-access learning center that could be posted and made available to other students and teachers.

The proposed framework for conducting evaluations has several implications for CALL evaluators. Many of these mark a significant change from current practices. For example, the suggested framework includes explicitly setting and reporting evaluation criteria and conducting a metaevaluation. Other evaluation tasks outlined may serve to reinforce already accepted practices such as identifying stakeholders and including them in designing the evaluation. These implications may also be helpful for stakeholders other than the evaluator. Stakeholders who are well informed about conducting reliable and valid evaluations can help evaluators conduct welldesigned evaluations. Administrators, publishers, designers, and others should strongly consider the following implications. Doing so will result in evaluations that are more systematic, thorough, and useful. Applying the evaluation tasks outlined in this paper might lead to the following suggestions for improving CALL evaluations. The list includes several variations from common trends in CALL evaluation to incorporate more practices from formal evaluators.

1. Evaluators should not limit themselves to CALL materials and activities a[6]s evaluands.

2. Evaluators have the responsibility to identify and determine the concerns or perspectives of all possible stakeholders. Looking at only one group (i.e., teachers, students, or developers) may not address all the issues considered in the evaluation.

3. Evaluators need to include stakeholders in articulating the purposes of evaluations. They need to consider their values and concerns.

---

[6]Chinnery, G.M. (2006) Going to the MALL: mobile assisted language learning. *Language Learning & Technology* 10(1): 9–16.

4. Evaluators should rely on the values of stakeholders as well as research to establish criteria used to evaluate the evaluand.

5. Evaluators should use research methods to conduct dependable and systematic evaluations.

6. Evaluation reports (publications, software reviews) should be useful to their audiences.

7. Evaluators should continually evaluate their own evaluations throughout the entire process.

8. Academic journals that publish CALL evaluations should adhere to evaluation standards such as the Program Evaluation Standards (2011) or develop their own to guide evaluators throughout the evaluation process and help determine the merit of worth of other evaluations.

In addition to these implications, CALL evaluators should make an effort to incorporate formal evaluator practices in their evaluation projects. While the framework is simple and the description limited, evaluators who use this in their evaluations will produce higher quality evaluations and benefit CALL.

CHAPTER II. PRACTICAL USAGE APPLICATIONS

2.1.The eight generic CALL applications

This chapter features eight generic CALL applications that together illustrate the breadth of what is available to CALL practitioners. While not intended to be exhaustive, this chapter includes sections on:

- Word processing
- Games
- Literature
- Corpus linguistics
- Computer-mediated communication (CMC)
- WWW resources
- Adapting other materials for CALL

Word processing

Word processing is the poor cousin of CALL. Almost all computers are sold with some version of word processing already installed, usually Microsoft *Word*. Such programs are widely used in the composition process. Within such word-processing packages, spelling and grammar checkers and simple thesaurus programs are standard tools.

There used to be only one way for learners to correct spelling on their own: using a dictionary. Now, as learners increasingly use computers in the composition process, they frequently do their spelling corrections with computer-based spelling checkers and seldom refer to a dictionary or use an online dictionary. Spelling checkers are also included in other applications such as database programs because as many as one in ten database queries fail because of spelling mistakes either in the query or within the database index itself (Smi[7]th, 1991).

After much research in the 1980s and early 1990s, attention has shifted away from the influence of spelling checkers and grammar checkers. However, it is an area which continues to merit attention as learners turn away at younger ages from writing on paper to computer-based composition.

Although computer software manufacturers may consult educators, most word-processing programs and other applications are designed not for school use, with attendant pedagogical concerns, but for business environments where learning is less important, or even completely unimportant.

This is particularly seen in programs that offer spelling correction but do not provide any

---

[7] Figueredo, L. and Varnhagen, C.K. (2006) Spelling and grammar checkers: are they intrusive? *British Journal of Educational Technology* 37(5): 721–32.

definitions. Learners – particularly second-language learners – frequently misspell a word then choose the first correction offered, without considering whether it is appropriate or not. Moreover, word-processing programs do not record misspellings or give any feedback to learners interested in reviewing their errors. Even worse, spelling checker programs allow learners to add new words to standard dictionaries and sometimes these words are themselves misspellings.

Word-processing programs also provide grammar support, although such support is sometimes of questionable worth. The grammar checker

included with various versions of Microsoft *Word*, for example, is preprogrammed to object to the use of the passive voice, even when the passive voice is appropriate. This and other rules can be suppressed within the program but it may be difficult for learners to do so and would require that they have a certain level of grammatical sophistication to appreciate why it might be done.

Beyond word processing, software such as Microsoft *Word* is increasingly multi-purpose. For example, it is commonly used by teachers (and sometimes learners) for creating semi-authentic learning materials featuring text, tables and illustrations as well as simple websites.

Games. Most educational games, or games used for pedagogical purposes, make use of a form of subversive teaching; learners are unaware of the objectives or, rather, do not share the same objectives as the teacher. Instead, learning takes place as an activity peripheral to play. Learners asked to play the board game *Monopoly*, for example, may not be aware that they are learning rudimentary concepts about the value of money and real estate, nor will they associate these concepts as part of learning objectives.

Similarly, learners are increasingly developers of digital content as online applications allow them to create and manipulate their own and others' media into videos, animations and games (see Alexander, 2008). Through such manipulation and development, learners acquire critical thinking and editing skil[8]ls.

However, to what degree can we measure the benefits of games? A related research question in this area is concerned with transfer: to what degree are skills learned in a game of use in the real world? The peripheral learning benefits in a game are likely to be small but are hopefully greater in a program devoted to some specific educational objective. The best educational games are those which embed the pedagogical objectives

---

[8] Oishi, L. (2007) Working together: Google Apps goes to school. *Technology & Learning* 27(9): 46–7.

so that the learners' perceptions are of play, while the teachers' hidden objectives are still achieved.

A.C. Derycke, C. Smith and L. Hemery suggest: Some of the highest pedagogical objectives can only be achieved by employing group learning activities such as group problem solving, games, case studies, exchanges with real experts.

In other cases, learning materials which are not perceived as being gamelike by the teacher may be perceived as such by the learner. For example, Nord describes an exchange with his students at Nanzan University in Nagoya, Japan in which they asked for another session in the Computer-

Assisted Language Learning (CALL) Laboratory using a particular game. Nord was confused until he realized that the game they were referring to was actually a traditional grammar drill (J.R. Nord, private communication, 1998).

The idea of *game* rests in the perception of the user, not the description of the developer, the pedagogical model or the label used by the teacher.

While entertainment applications have certainly increased general computer literacy and served to make computers more familiar and less threatening to the average young person, a question that needs to be addressed is: To what degree do young learners transfer their computer skills and enthusiasm to more academic learning at the computer? It may be that young learners' familiarity with the possibility of what computers are capable of makes them less tolerant of educational applications that do not match the average computer game's exciting presentation of information.

A degree of excitement is necessary in computer-based learning materials, particularly in the case of young learners who lack motivation for learning.

Young learners may seldom see beyond the moment to consider the consequences of their learning (or not learning) something. Young learners can perhaps be cajoled into learning through the threat of tests, but cannot easily assess the importance of year-end grades, distant graduation or future employment. Within the classroom environment, computers can help in motivation through the organization of learning into game-like formats.

On the simplest level, the computer is a suitable game player as it can provide clues, levels of difficulty and rewards for solutions through points or visual stimulation. Most importantly, the computer is endlessly patient and never grows bored. Simple computer games include variations of many of those found in the real world. Example 4.1 Hangman

Hangman is a game that has long had a slightly morbid fascination for children learning English. In the paper-based version, a scaffold for a public hanging is drawn over a series of dashes representing the number and positions of letters in the target word. As the learner playing the game guesses, letters are filled in their correct places or body parts (head, torso, arms, legs) are drawn on a person in the hangman's noose. Players who can complete the word before the entire body is completed win, those who can't, lose. In computer-based versions of this game, the hanging is

Commercial quiz software. Particularly online, computer-based games are quizzes which test knowledge more than they teach it. Like games, quizzes are very motivating for learners as they appear to illustrate a learner's progress and give some security against fear of more formal exams. As computerbased quizzes are often done outside of class and not marked by teachers, learners may feel less threatened.

In these computer-based cloze programs, learners choose a text from a menu (for example, after an introductory paragraph) at selected intervals; every second to every ninth word. Deleted words are replaced with numbered blanks. Learners can request clues in the form of single letters. Such programs encourage careful reading but frustration may occur as the programs do not accept synonyms; usually learners must guess the exact word that has been deleted.

Literature. One of the ways in which learners are presented with opportunities to acquire language is through activities peripheral to the study of literature and other disciplines. A work of literature is not a simulation, but it has a high degree of fidelity, or authenticity, in that the learning materials are both extensive and taken from real-world sources. Literature forms the basis of many CALL programs.

Animated with a walk to the scaffold and loser messages such as 'Sorry!

You failed to save him.'

Despite the popularity of this game, teachers need to consider its appropriateness in the second-language classroom where some immigrant students

may be fleeing repressive governments where public hangings, perhaps of relatives, were commonplace.

http://www.allmixedup.com/hangman

Slater (1987) offer four main justifications for the use of literature in the language classroom: valuable authentic material, cultural enrichment, language enrichment and personal involvement. They also note the place of non-fictional authentic materials, such as bus schedules. J. Collie and S. Slater suggest:

The same way that a bus ticket or an advertisement might be, literature can nonetheless incorporate a great deal of cultural information.

A rich source of content for CALL programs is literature which has come into the public domain and is freely available in digital formats, often with accompanying visual materials. This allows learners to manipulate text and comment on it in interesting ways. Farabaugh (2007), for example, talks about how students can use wikis to make sense of a Shakespeare play: commenting, editing comments and generally building their own knowledge base with personal opinion and other sources. J. Collie and S. Slater on the use of literature in language learning:

Collie and Slater (1987) use the term cultural enrichment to refer to the wealth of insights about other cultures (particularly the target language culture) that literature offers.

Skills in making inferences and deductions can be taught in different ways, but literature tends to teach them more naturally. In fact, many of the best CALL programs offer learning in the same way as good literature, presenting a narrative in which the reader learner draws a more general understanding of themes.

The relationship of literature to computer-based learning materials. Although Collie and Slater's (1987) observations on the link between language learning and literature were written with reference to traditional paper-based learning materials they also hold true for computer-based learning materials. However, there is a principal difference: computer based learning materials easily bridge the gap between fictional and non-fictional resources by routinely offering multimedia links between the two. In paper-based materials, this is sometimes found to a lesser degree in heavily annotated editions of literary works such as Shakespeare plays.

Hypertext and literature. Deegan and Sutherland (1990) note advantages of hypertext for both the study and writing of literature, arguing that texts and non-textual material are essentially fluid and easily manipulated, making it an ideal tool for showing the interconnection of ideas. G.P. Landow on the advantages of hypertext as a tool for learning *connectiveness* in literature:

The sheep like behavior displayed by many freshmen is often due to their having little information and little idea of what to do with it. One cannot make connections between fact A and six other facts if one knows only fact A. This lack of factual knowledge leads to reductive thinking. Additional information, however, will not help students think critically unless they have techniques for relating facts to each other. College liberates because it provides students with facts and offers examples of the way they can make connections for themselves. Intellectual freedom derives from an ability to make choices.

Whether or not learners use hypertext to make their own connections in literature and whether it helps in their general acquisition of language is an area of research worth investigating.

Corpus linguistics. Corpus linguistics is an important area in its own right within applied linguistics, but it is also a useful tool for the teaching and learning of language at the computer. This section outlines some of the key aspects of corpus linguistics and concordancing before going on to explain their applications to CALL.

The *corpus* in *corpus linguistics* refers to a body of text. The text can be made up of different examples of spoken or written language or a combination of both. Corpora (corpora = plural of corpus) can be based on simple and brief texts on a narrow topic or run into the millions of words, such as the British National Corpus (*http://www.natcorp.ox.ac.uk*), a 100-million word corpus of British English. Corpora can be unformatted text made up of individual words or formations. Alternatively, these can be tagged for grammatical functions or for other functions.

Simple searches can be used to count the frequency of different words and structures. To access, or make use of, a corpus, one uses a *concordancer* to look at

language patterns. A concordancer is a tool that looks at individual words (nodes) or groups of words and lists them with their immediate contexts; usually the seven or eight words that come before and after but, in some cases, the entire sentence for each word. The term for describing this approach is *key word in context* (KWIK).

Using corpora in the classroom involves making use of a concordancing program's ability to spot patterns and exceptions in language use.

Corpus linguistics in the classroom. Both teachers and learners can use corpus linguistics in various ways within the classroom.

A teacher might collect a set of student assignments and use a concordancing program to analyse examples of learners' language looking for typical error patterns. Systematic errors in learners' writing can be used as a basis for the development of learning materials. Alternatively, a teacher might look through established corpora of texts by native speakers of the target language and find examples for patterns and present these to learners as examples or adapt them into exercises.

Learners themselves can be trained in the use of a concordancing program (St John, 2001) and corpora, then become their own researchers finding examples and developing their own rules for grammatical structures, idioms and general usage, for example, investigating the differences between the verbs *look* and *see*. This approach is often called Data Driven Learning (DDL).

Data Driven Learning (DDL) is an inductive approach to learning in which learners acquire an understanding of language patterns and rules by becoming more involved in researching corpora, usually through the use of a computer-based concordancing program. Instead of studying patterns and rules, learners natura[9]lly internalize them. This approach can stimulate learners' interest in language and give them a sense of

---

Clark, R.E. (1985b) Evidence for confounding in computer-based instruction studies: analysing the meta-analyses. *Educational Communications and Technology Journal* 33(4): 249–62.

empowerment and responsibility for their own language education.

Computer-mediated communication. *Communicating using the computer* is often referred to as computer mediated communication (CMC) and is one of the more popular activities associated with CALL. CMC encompasses communication by email, bulletin boards, chat lines, within MOO (Multi-user domains, Object Oriented) environments and using social networking services such as *Face Book* and *Twitter*.

CMC refers to a situation in which computer-based discussion may take place but without necessarily involving learning. Of course, opportunities for learning are inherently present, especially in situations in which second-language learners need to engage in negotiation of meaning with native speakers of the target language or even with peers of non-native proficiency.

Email. Email is among the most popular uses of the Internet and presents many opportunities to enhance learning. From the teacher's perspective, one of the great advantages of email over some other forms of communication is the record of both one's own messages and the messages one receives. Using email, learners can communicate with peers, teachers and native speakers. Messages can be structured around an assignment in which the learner solicits special information, shares information about assignments (especially in a jigsaw format, sharing information with peers) or submits thoughts, questions and assignments to a teacher. However, communication with native speakers can be difficult if the learner provides input with substantial spelling and grammatical errors. Most email programs now come with rudimentary spelling checkers but teachers concerned about the quality of their students' writing may encourage them to compose their messages in a word-processing software program then copy and paste it into their email messages.

Asynchronous refers to communication that takes place at different times, for example, through email in which a message is sent and may be read at leisure by the recipient. Synchronous refers to communication that takes place at the same time, such as through chat lines. There are advantages to both modes. An asynchronous email allows the writer to take time to consider and compose a message, and messages can be processed when the interlocutor is ready – an important consideration when the communication is across different time zones.

Net pals. One informal use of email is for the establishment of email pen pals. Such pen pals or pen friends are sometimes called *net pals*. Ideally, net pal communication is between someone learning the target language and a native speaker of the target language living in the culture of the target language.

For example, a Nepalese student learning German might correspond with a native German-speaker living in Berlin. The advantage to the learner is that the native speaker is likely to offer extensive examples of authentic language, probably pitched at the appropriate age level of the language learner.

In practice, however, both parties can find net pal relationships frustrating. Native speakers may feel they cannot communicate effectively with the learner and may feel the learner has nothing to offer in return in the exchange. The language learner may find that slang, idioms, misspellings and typos interfere with comprehension. Net pals work best when both parties have extrinsic motivation (e.g., a common interest in football or visiting one another's countries) and where the language learner has good clarification strategies and/or the support of a language teacher.

Chat lines. A chat line is more technically known as *Internet Relay Chat* (IRC) and appears on-screen as a window that presents what the learner is writing in one pane while general discussion among other participants continues in another. Once the learner has completed a message and presses the *send* command, the message is queued and appears in the main pane as quickly as the modem and host computer allow. In some older programs, it is necessary to press the *reload* or *refresh* button to update to the latest message.

Concept 4.3 R U ready 2 GA?

The speed of discussion on chat lines challenges many learners' typing skills, so a series of abbreviations and emotives (sideways faces made through the use of type characters) are used to take the place of commonly used phrases.

An online conversation might follow along these lines.

John, IMHO, it's NBD that I can't CU tonite. We had FTF yesterday and

U were:). If you were:) B4, you shouldn't be :'-(now. TTYL. Janet.

:) a happy face

:'-(a crying face

2 to

4 for

ABT about

B4 before

BW best wishes

CU see you

FTF face to face

FYR for your reference

GA go ahead

Teaching and researching com 72 puter-assisted language learning

IMHO in my humble opinion

IOW in other words

LOL laugh out loud

NBD no big deal

POV point of view

R are

TTYL talk to you later

U you

Bulletin boards. Bulletin boards on which learners (both teachers and users) can post messages to be read later by others are built into some CALL environments

and more general learning platforms such as *Blackboard Vista*. In

such platforms, users can post messages and comment on the original posting and subsequent comments ad infinitum (see Concept 9.2).

Bulletin board. The advantage of bulletin boards over email is that the messages are shared with a broader community (a few select people, a class or the whole world) and comment can be more considered as readers have more time.

However, in some cases, when two or more people are actively responding to the same posting, communication can resemble a chat li[10]ne.

Netiquette, flaming and emotives. In online chat line discussions, email and on bulletin boards, there are certain rules of etiquette, or *netiquette*, to be followed. These rules cover issues such as the length of postings and technical issues (such as not including the entire message or string of messages to which you are responding), privacy issues (such as posting other people's email addresses without permission) and so on.

One of the most commonly abused of these netiquette rules is *flaming*.

---

[10] Coe, M. (1996) *Human Factors for Technical Communicators*. New York: Wiley.

Flaming is responding inappropriately to others. Flaming can include the use of ALL CAPS (the equivalent of online shouting), personal insults, excessive sarcasm and other behaviours that one might avoid, or at least temper with ironic expressions or tones, were one speaking in person. One way of tempering one's comments online is through the use of emotives, symbols made up of alphanumeric characters to form sideways-viewed faces: a smiling face :) a face sticking out a tongue :! A face expressing surprise :o

4.5.3 MOO, MUA, MUD, MUG, MUSH

Concept 4.5 MOO, MUA, MUD, MUSH, MUG

MOO: Multi-user domains, Object Oriented

MUA: Multi-User Adventure

MUD: Multi-User Domains/Dungeons

MUG Multi-User Game

MUSH: Multi-User Shared Hallucination

MOO, MUA, MUD, MUSH and MUG generally refer to the same thing (and are referred to hereafter as *MOO*), an online environment where moveable objects represent things and people. MOO objects may be photo-realistic 3-D manipulated models or 2-D flat representations. This environment is a synchronous online multi-user space, that is, action takes place in real time among several participants who put their characters into the same scene on a computer screen. These scenes are usually referred to as rooms and can have great visual interest. For example, 'rooms' can be seaside settings featuring lighthouses and surprisingly active sea life or depictions of castles in the air.

1. Introduce the students to the basics of MOOing. Take the class to a MOO in small groups and have them communicate with each other so they get used to the unique environment.

2. Collect the first drafts of an essay from the students (via hard copy or email). Have a copy of the draft with you for reference during the conference (either printed out or on-screen in a separate window).

3. Set up conferences for each student. Ask the students to bring three questions regarding their essay to the conference.

4. Meet each student at the MOO to discuss the draft, focusing on the questions they bring.

5. Through non-verbal gestures, encourage the student to do most of the 'talking'.

6. Lead the students to state clearly by the end of the conference what they will focus on during the revision process.

7. Have the students save a log of the conversation on their hard drive or portable storage device (e.g. USB), or do it yourself and send it to the student in an email message.

The advantages of such environments to learning a language is that a learner can enter into an environment where a target language is being spoken and he or she is forced to react to others' words and actions.

MOOs seem a promising direction for further research and materials development although the cognitive overhead of learning how to operate within such an environment may be daunting for some teachers and learners.

WWW resources. One of the more popular language-learning sites on the WWW was created by Dave Sperling, a California-based teacher who started Dave Sperling's ESL Cafй as a class project in 1995. His students' efforts attracted the attention of other learners and their queries lead naturally into providing information.

The website now serves as a portal, providing a directory of other CALL and

general language-learning resources.

Dave Sperling’s ESL Cafй: *http://www.eslcafe.com*

Several examples have already been given of opportunities for learning language using the WWW. The WWW has also presented opportunities for the creation of commercial websites dedicated to the teaching and learning of English. Such sites may have different foci in terms of age, level or even profession. For example, websites for improving business writing are popular.

Many such websites are driven by commercial concerns. Typically, the learner pays a fee for enrolling and taking online lessons or endures advertising, much of which will be targeted at the learners by, for example, textbook publishers, language schools and language testing services. Several publishers also maintain educational websites featuring portions of their work or extra study materials for their work.

Augmenting a textbook *Sounds Good*, a book series by the author of this book, has an interactive website with additional materials and quizzes tied to each unit of the series.

The website provides extra materials that students using the book – or anyone else – can make use of. Listening passages feature interactive tests that are automatically corrected. The website also features 48 MP4 podcasts which allow the student to listen to a conversation while the text automatically scrolls on the MP4 player screen.

Other resources commonly found on the WWW include those created by learners and teachers. These include everything from software to class handouts and presentations in the form of PowerPoint files. These resources vary in quality and extent but at least have the virtues of being free and easy to find with a search engine.

Many websites, especially those associated with government and nonprofit organizations, such as Greenpeace (*www.greenpeace.org*) create associated websites to cater to students and language learners. These may also have professional and informative free materials included for teachers.

Club Penguin. Club Penguin is an interesting example of a virtual environment where children can play and interact safely. A child creates a free account, picks a name and a colour for his or her penguin. Parents can choose the level of security of the chat experience in which the child is involved. An 'Ultimate Safe-Chat', which allows users to converse using a list of common greetings, questions and answers. There is also a more standard chat mode with filters to help monitor profanity and bullying. The penguin avatars explore many rooms and environments including a cafй, a pet store and a disco. Almost every area on the site features games to play.

http://www.clubpenguin.com/parents

Adapting other materials for CALL. Besides materials especially targeted for language learning, there are many materials which can be adapted. Many games and simulations not intended for language learning can be adapted for such a purpose, particularly for advanced learners, as they are likely to be rich in authentic language.

SimCity (i.e. simulated city) is one of many programs from Maxis which offer interactive simulations.

The first *SimCity* was created in 1989 and has influenced many other so-called 'god games' in which one organizes and influences events in a simulated world. In the case of *SimCity*, the user is a mayor or city manager who makes decisions on how a city should be built. The game teaches some basic economics as the user reconciles additions to the community which The Sims 2: Double Deluxe © 2010 Electronic Arts Inc. The Sims is a trademark or registered trademark of Electronic Arts Inc. in the U.S. and/or other countries.

generate income (e.g. a toxic waste dump) with problems (e.g. increased pollution). Each solution seems to have an attendant disadvantage and the user is constantly petitioned by fictional citizens protesting and making requests. There are also virtual newspapers which influence events and various meetings one must attend. The program continues to be updated and, in 2008, was adapted for the iPhone platform.

Maxis has produced many Sim games for environments ranging from jungles to other planets. The most interesting recent development has been the release of a program called *The Sims*. In this game, users create characters and their families, build homes and cater to their needs (e.g. hunger). If one clicks on a fridge, the character on screen will go to the fridge and prepare a meal for himself/herself. Many users model their own families and homes in the program.

A more recent development is *Spore*, a game in which a player controls the development of a single-celled organism into a complex thinking being, ostensibly controlling the creature's evolution. The game has been criticized for placing entertainment far above sound scientific principles but it is an example of a game that involves a great deal of reading and discussion if played with more than one person.

The Sims: *http://thesims.ea.com*

Spore: *http://www.spore.com/f*

Many other materials on the WWW are easy to adapt for classroom learning and offer a rich source of authentic text, images, sound and video.

For example, a learner studying Japanese can go to countless websites on different topics of interest related to Japan to learn more about culture or information related to Japanese for Specific Purposes.

Learners can also visit online newspapers for the target language they are studying.

Personal Digital Assistants (PDAs) and mobile telephones

Bleeding Edge - is a pun on *Leading Edge* and refers to a concern in educational computing and computing in general: the cost of buying the latest hardware and software.

New hardware and software is constantly being introduced and short term profit is often a greater consideration than reliability. This is especially true in the case of untried products which may not gain wide acceptance.

Apple introduced the Newton PDA in 1993 but discontinued production five years later.

Although it was the first PDA, it did not endure. Essentially, it was a bleeding edge development that was replaced by new PDAs which were eventually, in turn, replaced by the integration of Internet functions into mobile telephones, such as the *Blackberry*. Initially the principle entry method was through writing on-screen with a stylus, but now miniature keys are more common, particularly as people have become assimilated to them through non-PDA type mobile phones.

Teachers need to be concerned about investing time and money in unproven technology but, at the same time, want to have current software and hardware that will not be soon outdated. This is particularly a concern as educational authorities often are happy to budget for computer labs but less enthusiastic about budgeting for services and upgrades.

A Personal Digital Assistant (PDA) is a small hand-held computer for downloading and storing information such as documents, databases and calendar entries. It is less powerful than a desktop or laptop computer, but less expensive and more portable. Portability is achieved by eliminating the keyboard and minimizing the screen size. PDAs have largely been replaced in the marketplace with mobile telephones that share many of the same functions and often feature Internet connectivity.

***Graffiti* handwriting software.** In Ray Bradbury's (1958) collection of science-fiction short stories, *The Martian Chronicles*, one tale tells of a man who finds an alien's deserted home that miraculously adapts to his needs for water and shelter. However, the home soon grows tired of adapting and instead transforms the man into one of its original occupants: an overgrown lizard. It is a suitable metaphor for the computer's tendency to impose its style and affordances (i.e. what the program is or appears to be capable of doing in terms of both intended and unintended functions) on users and this was the route taken by the designers of *Graffiti*, a handwriting recognition system.

In the absence of a keyboard, a major challenge to PDAs has been recognition of handwriting. Early models struggled to recognize individual handwriting but the creators of the *Graffiti* system realized it would be easier to make users adapt their handwriting to the PDA.

2.2. Criteria language teachers use when selecting computer-assisted language learning technologies

English is the www.englishtown.com which requires subscription to do the mini tests or to release various grammar exercises as download material for EFL students to print them. For example, the grammar test on 'conditionals' in this site provides the learners with immediate feedback after each question. Here again, the tests can be done either online or after printing them. However, you cannot ask for immediate feedback if you print the material. Vocabulary related Computer software such as guessing games, do-it-yourself dictionaries or word building activities provide a nice challenge for students. A word game program such as the Word Hunt or the site www, puzzlemaker.com enables the students to learn and practice vocabulary easily.

Other appliances, such as televisions, are becoming more computer connected

and each technological advance presents new opportunities for the delivery of CALL. New gaming platforms, such as the Nintendo *Wii*, offer tactile ways of interacting with computer programs and suggest learning opportunities for young children who find difficulty hunting and pecking at the keyboard or using a mouse pointing device. Brown (2008) notes the recent advances that have moved tactile computing forward, including addressing multiple-finger inputs that predict the obsolescence of the mouse pointer. This, virtual keyboards and speech recognition may help turn future computers into screens with no other peripheral input technologies. This has already been achieved on a small scale by applications such as the iPod *Touch* (see http://www.apple.com/ipodtouch/guidedtour).

One informal use of email is for the establishment of email pen pals. Such pen pals or pen friends are sometimes called *net pals*. Ideally, net pal communication is between someone learning the target language and a native speaker of the target language living in the culture of the target language.

For example, a Nepalese student learning German might correspond with a native German-speaker living in Berlin. The advantage to the learner is that the native speaker is likely to offer extensive examples of authentic language, probably pitched at the appropriate age level of the language learner.

In practice, however, both parties can find net pal relationships frustrating. Native speakers may feel they cannot communicate effectively with the learner and may feel the learner has nothing to offer in return in the exchange. The language learner may find that slang, idioms, misspellings and typos interfere with comprehension. Net pals work best when both parties have extrinsic motivation (e.g., a common interest in football or visiting one another's countries) and where the language learner has good clarification strategies and/or the support of a language teacher.

Although computer software manufacturers may consult educators, most word-processing programs and other applications are designed not for school use, with attendant pedagogical concerns, but for business environments where learning is less important, or even completely unimportant.

This is particularly seen in programs that offer spelling correction but do not provide any definitions. Learners – particularly second-language learners – frequently misspell a word then choose the first correction offered, without considering whether it is appropriate or not.

Moreover, word-processing programs do not record misspellings or give any feedback to learners interested in reviewing their errors. Even worse, spelling checker programs allow learners to add new words to standard dictionaries and sometimes these words are themselves misspellings.

Word-processing programs also provide grammar support, although such support is sometimes of questionable worth. The grammar checker

included with various versions of Microsoft *Word*, for example, is preprogrammed to object to the use of the passive voice, even when the passive voice is appropriate. This and other rules can be suppressed within the program but it may be difficult for learners to do so and would require that they have a certain level of grammatical sophistication to appreciate why it might be done.

Beyond word processing, software such as Microsoft *Word* is increasingly multi-purpose. For example, it is commonly used by teachers (and sometimes learners) for creating semi-authentic learning materials featuring text, tables and illustrations as well as simple websites.

The previously mentioned online music stores, as well as portable music players such as the iPod, have, for example, helped spurred the creation of CALL media aimed at casual learners. An example of this is the program *Earworms*, named after the German term *Ohrwurm*, which refers to a repetitive snippet of music that gets stuck in one's head. In each of *Earworms'* several language programs (12 at present), one listens to key words, phrases and simple dialogues along with pneumonic devices repetitively thrown back and forth by a male English speaker and a female speaker of the target language over a musical background. The intention is for the learner to attend to the program passively, playing the music and dialogues as background audio, while doing other things, such as household chores.

But, a larger part of the changes that have occurred are grouped under the *Web 2.0* moniker for a collection of technologies aimed at enhancing creativity and collaboration, particularly through social networking.

Biographical contact pages like *My Space* and *Facebook* have served to give millions of technological opportunity to share content about themselves from their music preferences, to personal diary entries; we now live in an age where everyone with a personal computer and an Internet connection can be an international publisher. The video-sharing service *YouTube* has similarly presented opportunities for individuals and organizations to become directors and producers and post both their favourite videos (sometimes illegally) and their own videos. *Web*

2.0 is notable for encouraging a move away from static personal websites to interactive blogging and from expert-generated taxonomies to individual-created *folksonomies*, the latter term referring to collaboratively built websites such as *Wikipedia*, where the public creates, contributes to and edits the content of the site. *Wikis*, community-edited websites on any topic, are a new way to create and organize knowledge. A more involved editorial and creative role for some web users comes in the form of *mashups*.

Assisted Language Learning (CALL) Laboratory using a particular game. Nord was confused until he realized that the game they were referring to was actually a traditional grammar drill (J.R. Nord, private communication, 1998). The idea of *game* rests in the perception of the user, not the description of the developer, the pedagogical model or the label used by the teacher. While entertainment applications have certainly increased general computer literacy and served to make computers more familiar and less threatening to the average young person, a question that needs to be addressed is: To what degree do young learners transfer their computer skills and enthusiasm to more academic learning at the computer? It may be that young learners' familiarity with the possibility of what computers are capable of makes them less tolerant of educational applications that do not match the average computer game's exciting presentation of information.

A degree of excitement is necessary in computer-based learning materials, particularly in the case of young learners who lack motivation for learning.

Young learners may seldom see beyond the moment to consider the consequences of their learning (or not learning) something. Young learners can perhaps be cajoled into learning through the threat of tests, but cannot easily assess the importance of year-end grades, distant graduation or future employment. Within the classroom environment, computers can help in motivation through the organization of learning into game-like formats.

CONCLUSION

In this paper, we have reviewed the popular CALL frameworks and formal evaluation tasks and illustrated the gap between formal evaluation and CALL evaluation. Our proposal to implement formal evaluation practices into CALL evaluation may help provide evaluations that address several issues that have been overlooked in CALL evaluation. The field of CALL needs to be more aware of the practices in mainstream evaluation and apply them when evaluating 40 CALL materials and activities. Formal evaluators and publications have much to offer CALL. CALL evaluation publications should reflect the expertise that experienced evaluators bring to evaluation and be based on principles similar to those to which formal evaluators espouse.

From here, there are several questions regarding CALL evaluation that may need to be addressed. First, how might this proposed framework benefit CALL publications including peer reviewed research and software reviews? Many publications in top tier CALL journals publish peer-reviewed research regarding the efficacy of author-generated CALL materials or CALL 39 activities. While some may argue that evaluation and research are similar, future research and initiatives regarding appropriateness of such publications would be helpful. Or in other words, should research that is essentially evaluation be portrayed as research? How does the evaluation of author-generated products benefit CALL in terms of the body of research it aims to contribute to? Similarly, the current conventions for software reviews in these same top-tier journals need to be evaluated. How effective are these published reviews? As outlined in the article, our proposed framework for CALL evaluation includes essential tasks that are missing from popular CALL evaluation frameworks. Software reviews that follow our proposed framework will provide more information to readers and make them more readily usable by those same readers.

Carefully identified stakeholders can provide essential information about the evaluand and help shape the evaluation in such a way that it becomes useful to all those invested.Key authors in CALL have identified possible stakeholders for CALL evaluations. Levy and Stockwell (2006) discussed how designers and developers of CALL materials are evaluators. They pointed out that many of the published CALL research articles focus on tools and their evaluation. They stated, “the designer-evaluator perspective is a very important one incontemporary CALL evaluation” (p. 52). Chapelle (2001) argued that due to the complexity of CALL evaluation, all those who use CALL should be involved in the evaluation process. In a later article, Chapelle (2007) discussed audiences for evaluations. Regardless of the differences between stakeholders and audience, there is some overlap. She identified insiders, informed critics, and outsiders as three separate audiences. Insiders include software developers and other CALL researchers. Other teachers, learners, other applied linguists, and program decision makers are among the informed critics. Outsiders may overlap with critics and include program and policy decision makers. Hubbard (1988, 1996, 2006, 2011) gave high priority to teachers and learners as stakeholders. While these prominent figures in the field have identified a myriad of possible stakeholders, many published evaluations still focus on only one or two groups of stakeholders.

Separate from the previous questions regarding the role of evaluation in published literature, CALL evaluators should consider the used of evaluation standards. Is there a need for standards or guidelines similar to those proposed in the field of formal evaluation or would currently adopted formal evaluation standards such as the Joint Committee on Standards for Educational Evaluation be sufficient for CALL evaluations? Regardless of the answer to this question, it needs to be asked and studied, and the field of CALL should look to the field of evaluation for guidance and understanding.

This chapter looked at different CALL applications. The main point is that there are many diverse ways of approaching CALL and new ways, such as the use of PDAs, are being developed. One measure of the success of any of the applications mentioned in this chapter is the amount of work they require on the part of the teacher and learner before language learning begins. If the cognitive overhead is too high, then the technology, however wonderful, may not be worth the investment of time by teachers and learners.

This chapter looked at the history of CALL, highlighting several developments of hardware and software and noted how the arrival of desktop computers prompted more teacher-led research. In general, a lot of CALL software is stuck in a behaviourist rut partly because offering a behaviourist mode of instruction is an easy thing for computers to do. Developments in web technologies are presenting teachers and learners with simple tools to fashion a new generation of learning experiences.

This study was the first in-depth review to examine the status, trends, and particularly the thematic structure of CALL research during 1995–2019 using a STM-based bibliometric strategy. Results revealed that technology played an important role in facilitating FLE throughout all stages. CALL began expanding from limited applications, such as multimedia in the early stages, to a growing number of technologies (e.g., mobile technologies, CMC, and ASR) in the middle stages, to finally the diverse applications and tools including DMC, wikis, VW/VR, and digital games presently being applied. The use of these diverse applications in language education is encouraged by pedagogical and technological advances. The development and advance of sensor and networking technologies and Web 2.0, as well as the pedagogy needed for ubiquitous, immersive, blended, and collaborative learning, was shown to contribute to the increasing application of advanced technologies to facilitate language learning. Although various new technologies (e.g., mobile technologies, VW/VR, digital games, CMC, DMC, and wikis) are evident in the CALL literature, the application of the very latest technological advances remains limited. With the increasing prevalence of personalized learning, CALL scholars are advised to stay abreast of the latest AI technological trends, such as deep learning and LA, and explore how to integrate them into language classrooms to construct knowledge, develop critical thinking, and promote better learning outcomes.

For future studies, further research can be conducted on the effectiveness of classroom writing and collaborative writing via Google Docs in motivating students. Since the majority of the students in this study felt that learning through technology has improved their quality of writing, then getting them to work together beyond thc classroom environment would be much easier, time-saving and facilitate students' learning. Other educational technologies can also be used to compare with Google Docs to investigate students' motivation level. Students can acquire lots of support when technology is used more in language classrooms. However, teachers must also remember that students still prefer a balance between the use of technology and classroom teaching so blended learning would be another teaching method that can be explored further to enhance language teaching and learning.

Acknowledgment. We would like to take this opportunity to thank God Almighty, our families, friends and the management of our institute, for their continuous support and encouragement throughout our journey in completing this research. Also, not forgetting our amazing students who participated in this research and gave us their cooperation to enable us to complete the research successfully.

GLOSSARY

Among the most popular computer-based testing programs is Question mark's

Perception

(*http://www.qmark.com/uk/home.htm*). The program works within some other programs, such as *Blackboard Vista* (see Concept 9.2) and offers a wide variety of ways of evaluating learner performance and the use of banks of items to help individualize tests over repeated attempts. A similar popular program is *Respondus* (see *http://www.respondus.com*).

• **Drag-and-drop:** the learner answers by dragging and dropping up to 10

graphics into position.

• **Essay question:** the learner answers by typing up to 30,000 characters

of text. Correct and incorrect answers can be defined in advance by entering a list of acceptable answers. A logic feature can score based on the presence or absence of keywords or key phrases and the text saved for later consideration by a teacher.

• **Fill-in-the-blank:** the learner is presented with a statement where one or more words are missing and completes the missing words; multiple words can be listed as acceptable including misspelled words.

• **Hotspot:** a learner clicks on a picture to indicate a choice.

• **Likert scale:** the learner selects one choice from choices such as 'strongly agree' through 'strongly disagree' that are weighted with numbers to aid analysis of the results.

-Survey Monkey (see *http://www.surveymonkey.com*) is among the most popular of online survey instruments with a wide scope for personalization and data collection.

It is easy to use and administer. There are free alternatives also available on the WWW, including Free Online Surveys (see *http://freeonlinesurveys.com*). Online surveys have the advantage of being easy to freely distribute to large numbers of people. However, the immediacy of such survey technology should be mixed with cautions against sending out rushed surveys that contain errors or may raise ethical issues. All such surveys need to be carefully piloted with a small group first.

• **Matching:** two lists of statements/words are presented and the learner

must match items.

• **Matrix:** this question type presents several multiple choice questions

together where the learner selects one choice for each statement or question presented. This question type is used to cross-relate responses from

a single item.

• **Multiple choice:** the learner selects one choice from up to 40 possible

answers. There is no limit to the length of each answer.

• **Multiple response:** similar to multiple choice except the learner is not

limited to choosing one response; he or she can select none, one or more

of the choices offered.

• **Numeric questions:** a learner is prompted to enter a number that is

scored as an exact answer with another score if the response is within a

range.

• **Pull-down list (selection question):** a series of statements are presented and the learner can match these statements to a pull-down list.

• **Ranking (rank in order):** a list of choices must be ranked numerically.

• **Select-a-blank:** the learner is presented with a statement where a word

is missing and words can be selected from a pull-down list to indicate

the answer.

• **True/False:** the learner selects 'True' or 'False' in response to a question.

• **Word response (text match):** the learner types in a single word, or a

few words, to indicate the answer.

• **Yes/No:** the learner selects 'Yes' or 'No' in response to the question.

(adapted from *http://www.qmark.com/uk/perception/index.htm*)

Table - 1

***Top Discriminating Terms for Each Topic* Labels**	**Representative terms**
DMC	dmc, identity, networking, community, gaming, fan, digital, project, space, socialization, intercultural, situated, site, science, engagement, affordances, literacy, urban, construction, social
MALL	mobile, anxiety, achievement, device, phone, attitude, motivation, flipped, mall, courseware, mobile-assisted, game-based, elementary, ubiquitous, smart, app, adaptive, efl,

	esp, context-aware technology, self-directed, heritage, adoption, computer, family, teaching, professional, project-based, use, french, laboratory, methodology, need, technological, become, field, style, university, innovative
PBL	blog, course, forum, blogging, reflective, undergraduate, cultural, blended, thinking, culture, metacognitive, discussion, class, semester, journal, questionnaire, enrolled, online, cross-cultural, project
blended learning	
multimedia	discrimination,

enhanced learning-audiovisual resources	training, e-books, vowel, exposure, treatment, improvement, forword, identification, audiovisual, temporal, listener, trained, week, production, av, high variability, lli, masking, talker
feedback and assessment	cf, feedback, corrective, correction, explicit, error, uptake, provision, received, correct, metalinguistic, audioblogs, grammatical, essay, grammar, structured, implicit, immediate, response, icall
multimedia enhanced learning-captions/subtitles	caption, subtitle, listening, captioning, comprehension, l1, video,

	l2, processing, pronoun, viewing, syntactic, test, organizer, reliance, clip, lexical, sentence, memory, resolution
seamless learning	deaf, preschool, seamless, sign, flashcard, collocation, emotion, ar, storybook, augmented, facial, home, image, phase, cfl, application, object, noun, technology-assisted, content
CMC and SCMC	scmc, dyad, interaction, negotiation, chat, synchronous, telecollaboration, cmc, recasts, computer-mediated, interactional, text-based, face-to-face,

	telecollaborative, communicative, communication, exchange, discourse, fluency, complexity
GBL	player, playing, game, idiom, contextual, warcraft, play, artificial, acquired, multiplayer, gameplay, variation, autism, parallel, action, statistical, network, adult, nssl, word
glosses/annotations and vocabulary learning	reading, vocabulary, annotation, reader, glossing, retention, presentation, dictionary, gloss, mode, load, cognitive, format, character, multimedia, read, text, comprehension, hypermedia, verbal

wiki-based learning	wikis, writing, writer, wiki, keyboarding, corpus, collaborative, prewriting, search, composition, revision, write, mt, wiki-based, google, kong, hong, collaboration, wrs, wrote
digital books	story, literacy, girl, narrative, multimodal, robot, early, authenticity, nonverbal, author, boy, argues, medium, tutorial, act, child, digital, methodological, claim, book
ASR	asr, mispronunciation, detection, pronunciation, automatic, speech, agent, capt, utterance, tone, recognition, dialog, system, evaluation, articulator,

	locus, verify, classification, method, non-native
VW and VR	virtual, autonomy, world, sl, chatbot, autonomous, interest, recording, life, immersion, task-based, instant, telepresence, vr, messaging, immersive, reality, profile, weekly, partner

Table - 2

Abbreviations in the Main Text **Abbreviations**	**Full names**
CALL	computer-assisted language learning
ICTs	information and communication technologies
ASR	automatic speech recognition
MALL	mobilc-assistcd languagc learning
DGBLL	digital game-based language learning
TELL	technology-enhanced language learning
CMC	computer-mediated communication

FLE	foreign language education
GBL	game-based learning
NLP	natural language processing
AI	artificial intelligence
STM	structural topic modelling
M-K	Mann-Kendall
RQ	research questions
WoS	Web of Science
SSCI	Social Sciences Citation Index
SCI	Science Citation Index
ACP	average citations per article
H-index	Hirsch index
LLT	Language Learning & Technology
DMC	digital multimodal

	composing
SCMC	synchronous computer-mediated communication
VW	virtual world
VR	virtual reality
PBL	project-based learning
MEL	multimedia-enhanced learning
PLL	personalized language learning
LA	learning analytics

LIST OF REFERENCES

1. Boswood, T. (ed.) (1997) *New Ways of Using Computers in Language Teaching*. Arlington, VA: TESOL.

2. Boyd, G.M. and Mitchell, D.P. (1992) How can intelligent CAL better adapt to learners? *Computers Education* 18(1–3): 23–8.

3. Bush, M.D. (2008) Computer-assisted language learning: from vision to reality? *CALICO* 25(3): 443–70.

4. Bush, V. (1945) As we may think. *Atlantic Monthly*, 176(1): 101–8. Available at *http://www.theatlantic.com/doc/194507/bush*, accessed 1 December 09.

5. Chapelle, C. (1997) CALL in the year 2000: still in search of research paradigms. *Language Learning and Technology* 1(1): 19–38.

6. Chapelle, C. (2001) *Computer Applications in Second Language Acquisition:*

Foundations for Testing, Teaching and Research. Cambridge: Cambridge University Press. Chapelle, C. and Heift, T. (2009) Individual learner differences in CALL: the field independence/dependence (FID) construct. *CALICO* 26(2): 246–66.

7. Chapelle, C. and Jamieson, J. (1983) Language lessons on the PLATO IV System. *System* 11(1): 13–20.

8. Chapelle, C. and Jamieson, J. (1991) Internal and external validity issues in research on CALL effectiveness. *Computer-assisted Language Learning and Testing*. New York: Newbury House: 37–59.

9. Chapelle, C., Jamieson, J. and Park, Y. (1996) Second language classroom research traditions: how does CALL fit? In Pennington, M. (ed.), *The Power of CALL*. Houston, TX: Athelstan: 33–53.

10. Chaudron, C. (1988) *Second Language Classrooms: Research on Teaching and Learning.*

11. Chen, D. and Zhao, Y. (1997) Eweb and homepage maker: making it easier to develop content on the WWW. *Computer-Assisted Language Learning*; 10(5) (Nov): 427–41.

12. Chinnery, G.M. (2006) Going to the MALL: mobile assisted language learning. *Language Learning & Technology* 10(1): 9–16.

13. Chinnery, G.M. (2008) Biting the hand that feeds me: the case for e-language learning and teaching. *CALICO* 25(3): 471–81.

14. Chiu, T.-L., Liou, H.-C. *et al.* (2007) A study of web-based oral activities enhanced by automatic speech recognition for EFL college learning. *Computer-Assisted Language Learning* 20(3): 209–33.

15. Christensen, E., Merrill, P. and Yanchar, S. (2007) Second language vocabulary acquisition using a diglot reader or a computer-based drill and practice program. *Computer-Assisted Language Learning* 20(1): 67–77.

16. Clark, R.E. (1985a) Confounding in educational computing research. *Journal of Education Computing Research* 1(2): 137–48.

17. Clark, R.E. (1985b) Evidence for confounding in computer-based instruction studies: analysing the meta-analyses. *Educational Communications and Technology Journal* 33(4): 249–62.

18. Al-Sharari, M., & Al-Jamal, D. (2013). Involving parents in CALL: An empirical study. *Journal of Education and Practice, 4*(16), Retrieved on 12 April, 2016, from http://www.iiste.org/Journals/index.php/JEP/article/view/7367.

19. Coe, M. (1996) *Human Factors for Technical Communicators*. New York: Wiley.

20.Cohen, A.D. and Oxford, R. (in preparation) *Teaching and Researching Learning*

21. Cohen, A.D. (2007) Becoming a strategic language learner in CALL. *Applied Language Learning* 17: 57–71.

22.Yang, J. C., & Quadir, B. (2018). Effects of prior knowledge on learning performance and anxiety in an English learning online role-playing game. *Educational Technology & Society, 21*(3), 174–185.

23.Yang, J., Thomas, M. S., Qi, X., & Liu, X. (2019). Using an ANN-based computational model to simulate and evaluate Chinese students' individualized cognitive abilities important in their English acquisition. *Computer Assisted Language Learning, 32*(4), 366–397.

24.Yang, S. J., Ogata, H., Matsui, T., & Chen, N. S. (2021). Human-centered artificial intelligence in education: Seeing the invisible through the visible. *Computers and Education: Artificial Intelligence, 2*, 100008. https://doi.org/10.1016/j.caeai.2021.100008

25. Yuan, C., & Huang, Y.-C. (2020). Personalized sentence generation using generative adversarial networks with author-specific word usage. *Computación y Sistemas, 24*(1), 17–28..

26. Zhang, R., & Zou, D. (2020). Types, purposes, and effectiveness of state-of-the-art technologies for second and foreign language learning. *Computer Assisted Language Learning*, 1–47. https://doi.org/10.1080/09588221.2020.1744666

Internet sites:

27.

http://www.qmark.com/uk/perception/index.htm)

28.

http://www.iiste.org/Journals/index.php/JEP/articl

e/view/7367.

29. https://doi.org/10.1016/j.caeai.2021.100008

30.

https://doi.org/10.1080/09588221.2020.1744666

9 789369 081745

Printed at Repro India Ltd.